THE ULTIMATE
TEDDY BEAR
PHOTO ALBUM

Compiled by

D1304987

My favourite teddy bear

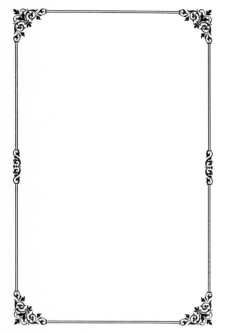

Old-fashioned humpback

- - - - - - - - - - - - - - - - - - -

Three little bears

- - - - - - - - - - - - - - - - - - -

A royal Russian

- - - - - - - - - - - - - - - - - - -

Little tartan ted

- - - - - - - - - - - - - - - - -

The biggest bear

- -

A bear from France

Wrapped up warmly

Dressed for dinner

What a cheeky grin!

A copy of a classic

Flower power teddy

A Christmas gift

Waving goodbye!

The college professor

Sheepskin "Edward"

OLD BEARS

"Alex" has amber, glass eyes, as do many early 1930s bears

World War II "Edward" is made from dyed brown sheepskin

"Mr Fluffy" is one of the first British teddies, made in 1923

Plump "Arthur van Gelden" is a big 1930s Dutch bear

Made in the early 1930s, cuddly "Colin" can squeak!

"Mr Jollyboy" is a bright blue example of a coloured 1930s British bear

"Ross" is a 1950 British bear, with levers on the back of his head to open and close his mouth

Unlike early German teds, British 1930s "Chummy" has no hump

Big-footed "Bing oh!", made in 1911, growls when he moves

"Friend Petz" is a classic old German bear, with boot-button eyes, a pointed muzzle, and a humpback

Peter's rolling eyes and bared teeth frightened children, so only a few of this 1925 bear sold

OLD BEARS

"Maximilian", made in 1905, sports a big green cravat

Three pocket-sized 1920s bears

Wide-eyed "Compton" is a 1920s British bear with joined-up claws

This brown bear was presented to "Teddy" Roosevelt's grandson

German 1927 "Claus" has beige plush fur, tipped with a rich cinnamon colour

Typically British "Bertie" has a very triangular head

An amazing 1915 somersaulting bear

"Chilli Pepper", from the 1940s, has a clockwork music-box wound by a key

"Miss Jessie Criddle" is a cheap 1930s bear from F. W. Woolworth

This early French bear has a gold button trademark

Wind up the 1915 Bing Skating Bear and he'll skate away

BEAR WEAR

Tiny teddy, dressed as Santa, has a mini ted in his toy sack

Sloane Ranger bears wear wax jackets and boots and live near Sloane Square in London

A 1960s teddy wears a fashionable tank top

One of the first dressed bears wears a knitted jacket with brass buttons

Bear from the 1960s is embroidered with flowers

Here's looking at you, Humphrey Beargart!

Three little bears dressed for dinner

Master Teddy, from 1915, has a red patch to match his necktie

A rare schoolboy bear, made in 1989, who is wearing a new leather satchel

This saucy Sailor Bear is dressed all in blue

Paddington Bear, from Michael Bond's stories, has a blue duffle coat

Bear Wear

"Aloysius" keeps warm in his check, beige scarf

Dressed to look just like Rupert Bear

"Watty Watford" bear wears stripy socks and a scarf

French bear wears a beret and an Eiffel Tower brooch

A teddy bear professor with a briefcase and mortarboard

"Alfonzo", in a Russian tunic, belonged to a princess

Sheepskin bear has red tartan dungarees

Bellhop Bear, in hotel livery

"Kensington", made in 1918, has a dazzling Indian jacket bought for him in the 1960s

Teddy from the 1930s wears fashionable Dutch trousers

Here comes the bridegroom with his beautiful bride all in white

MODERN BEARS

"Bobby Bear", made in 1955, has no feet!

"Felix" is a lifelike black bear from the late 1950s

Cute Cheeky from 1960 has bells in his big ears

A golden mohair copy of the 1909 teddy bear

A 1980 replica of a model bear made by famous bear manufacturer Richard Steiff

Teddy's humped back and long limbs caricature an old bear

Sir Mortimer is named after Sir Mortimer Wheeler, who excavated a Roman town near the bear artist's home

Red, white and blue teddy made for the coronation of Queen Elizabeth II in 1953

Machine-washable 1963 ted

Australian "Joycie" has no joints!

Popular, plain brown bear

An old-style bear, made in 1985, called "Knebbyworth"

Modern Bears

Floppy-eared Flash wears World War medals

In 1985, "Woody Herman" had his face and feet carved from smooth wood

"Darren" was made in 1975 and growls when he is tilted

"Horst" has a big head and an open mouth, like many 1950s bears

This bear was made by a special "bear artist" – Ginger T. Brame

American Freddie, from 1989, has a pointed muzzle and thin body like early teddy bears

Brian's Bear was made in 1987 for the first shop selling only teddy bears

Jackie-Baby is a bear cub from 1953

Shaggy, pink Teddy Rose looks like a 1920s bear

A golden-brown bare back

A 60th-birthday bear for British toy makers, Merrythought Ltd.

Based on a 1905 bear, except for the heart-shaped gold muzzle

Lace and pearl Bride from 1990

Sloane Rangers

Waving hello!

Master Teddy

The Queen's Coronation bear

Sail away with me

Hotel Bellhop

Little big-head

World War hero

An old British bear

The newlyweds

Bear in a bowtie

Threadbare teddy

Ready for school

A bear profile

Rupert Bear lookalike

A bear from Darkest Peru

Dark brown bear

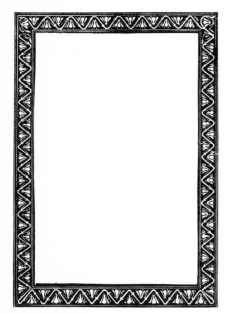

Famous movie star

"Aloysius"

Here comes the Bride